.

SOMEONE ELSE'S MEMOIRS

Other Books by Ron Charach from **Quarry Press**

The Big Life Painting

The Naked Physician:
Poems about the Lives of Patients and Doctors (Editor)

SOMEONE ELSE'S MEMOIRS

RON CHARACH

For Barbara
Warm regards
Ron Charach
T.R.'98

QUARRY
PRESS

The publisher gratefully acknowledges the assistance of The Canada
Council, the Ministry of Canadian Heritage, the Ontario Arts Council, and
the Ontario Publishing Centre.

The series "Eating Houses" first appeared in the Food issue of *Descant*
magazine. The series "Hecla Island," along with illustrations, was first
published by *Matrix*. Other poems have appeared in the journals *Arc,
Descant, event, Grain, The New Quarterly, Poet Lore, Prairie Fire, Viewpoints,*
and *The New England Journal of Medicine,* and in the League of Canadian
Poets Anthologies *More Garden Varieties* and *Vintage 93.*
    To paraphrase Winnicott's remark about infants, there is no such thing
as a poet. Helpful revisions of my work have been suggested by my wife
Alice Charach, and by visual artist / poet Andy Patton. Bob Hilderley put up
with endless changes; Colin Morton took a conservational approach to
editing and helped shape the manuscript. More occasional, but valued
suggestions came from poetry editors and poets Donna Bennett, Roo
Borson, Di Brandt, Kim Maltman, Nadine McInnis, Kenneth Radu, Rhea
Tregebov, and visual artist Janice Gurney.

Canadian Cataloguing in Publication Data

Charach, Ron
    Someone else's memoirs

Poems.
ISBN 1-55082-105-9

    I. Title.

PS8555.H39834865 1994   C811'.54   C94-900280-1
PR9199.3. C43865   1994

Cover photograph by Ron Charach.
Design Consultant: Keith Abraham.
Printed and bound in Canada by Webcom Limited, Toronto, Ontario.

Published by
Quarry Press, Inc.,
P.O. Box 1061, Kingston, Ontario K7L 4Y5.

for Alice, Nathaniel and Dorothy

CONTENTS

EATING HOUSES

HECLA ISLAND

THE FARE TO TRENTON

PROLOGUE

I Need a Large House

"There he goes again . . ."

Pounding the stairs to the third floor on all fours
to settle an image fever . . . it takes a cathedral wall
to dam up silence, absorb the snores of innocence,
the whoops and bellows of cartoon characters, hoots
and hollers of game show contestants;
most of all, twin streams of sunlight and water
pouring through windows and showerheads
to stir the concentrate that settles
by very early morning.

My wife complains:
"This house is too big for a family of four," too big to heat,
to clean — to populate.
She never knew me as "the rabbit"
in a house so confining rage ricocheted
off the bare skin

into rinsed jars, pickle-jars, mustard jars,
jars that once held Mayonnaise. The Jars, like father,
sturdy but tippable, hidden behind open doors by day
serving as family latrines by night,
to be emptied next morning.
Proverbial pisspots: *Lulu had a baby/ its name was Tiny Tim/
she put it in a pisspot/ to see if it could swim . . .*
The only real toilet was upstairs, darkly monitored
by our skeleton-tenant Bryna,
who never seemed to need one.

You opened doors slowly, never knowing
who you might interrupt — knock over!
Only sizzle versus nozzle sounds to guide you:
mother, father, brother,
united in cramped and hasty physiology.

Ron Charach

When a door swung open nearly all the way
and squatter's rights were not in play, the inevitable *clunk!*
of door striking jar, different notes
for empty or full, graded penalties, depending
on the pisser's rank.
But when doors were pushed in a dream
and the noise came back empty, and no golden stream
came seeping across the beaten hardwood floor,
relief soon changed to despair,
as small predictable spaces came into view
but absolutely refused
to unfold.

11

SEA
LOTION

Uncle Jake and the Cardgame on Earth

Not to detract from the ravishing bride
or the pale Bar Mitzvah boy with his fistful
of envelopes, But at every family affair
we take time out to honor Jake the Elder.
"Not that I'm good-looking like our young
master of ceremonies," he winks,
helped to his feet to toast
the proud parents.

Being the Elder
rented by branches of the family
for a holdover bottle of V.S.O.P.
and, though no thinker, great posture
for the eighty-two years
in a family of widows and shrunken men.
Two separate shocks, his white metallic hair
and the priceless gold pocket watch on a chain.
But Jake's eighty-two years parted down the middle
when Father took us down to the basement
to tell this:
"*My* father, your *Zaidy* Abraham,
who they called the Angel,
Alev Hasholem (may he rest in peace),
sent me out one night into the wind and snow
wearing my hooded jacket,
to ask your Uncle Jake for the money back
— from the 'business loan.'
I turn up out of a bitter winter wind
— Uncle's triplex — an upstairs steaming with men,
seven of Jake's cronies playing poker
for high stakes.
Shivering, my knock faint
on the oak door, like an intruder.
And there's Jake himself in a haze of cigarsmoke
sipping whiskey and ignoring me
— *white-haired even then!* —
holding his good hand close, a joker
among men who are feeling for kings.

Ron Charach

"What loan?" he laughs, throwing
another of Father's sawbucks
into the pile.

And so, "Go Home,"
It meant more black-bread-and-soup
or thinned soup. *"Go home!"* The years rewarmed anyway
because Mother was dead three years by then,
and the wrong brother gifted
with a poker face
in the Great Depression."

But why believe a bitter man like Dad,
when the family *needed* an Elder
to make up for its lack of history?
Besides, Father counted everything like coins;
he might have envied Jake's ace hand
of forty more years of robust life
still to come, card games no one invited Dad to,
even as a grown man.

Now they're both dead,
is it Heaven for Dad, wrestling Jake down,
their jackets off, suspender buckles snapping,
locking legs and grabbing each other by the hernias?
Dad pulling at that thick white hair like sun-bleached turf
trying to pry Jake from his marked cards,
toasted black bread falling all around them
thrown from the top of the tenement stairs
by *the Hooded Boy*
who would grow up all over *his* son,
compressing whatever mattered to the bottom line,
never taking chances —

"Jake the Snake" was more like it.
ACCORDING TO MY FATHER

A Photograph of Aydosha Malakovich

There were no color photographs of Aydosha Malakovich

or of you, Bryna, her sister who left the Old World
to wind up our upstairs tenant
overcharged by Dad for your English,
a family skeleton without a family.
Through parched lips and yellow teeth you swore
that Aydosha had been "the fat one"
of the five girls.

Mom had to write your letters back to Russia.
Squinting through badly broken English,
a depressive stoop wearing a black suit
even in the summer heat:
Dear Aydosha: How are your feet? I am fine.
(Years later Aaron can still do a perfect Bryna,
will sometimes begin his letters by inquiring
after the health of our feet.)

I am fine. Easy to ignore;
not like that blurry little print on your dresser,
cracked and whispering:
There are more of you, Bryna,
There is a home,
'America' means nothing . . .

Hissing at the racket we made
you would charge, waving your veiny arms
trying to scare the life . . .
poking your hollow face ahead
for a better view of just who
was afraid of who . . .

Ron Charach

Why should you deal with kids
when you'd only known your own kid-sister Aydosha
five short years?
No kid when you arrived
with a half-dozen words, already crouching
in the black box of memory.

Once, while the family was away
you came upon Hammy in his musty cage
in the summer-kitchen,
water-tower and squeaking wheel,
and *drowned* him *in a pickle-jar!*
"I thought he was a mouse . . ."
his bloated little body,
swollen face to the glass,
tiny feet held kangaroo-style
trying to ward off some
"Murderer! Murderer! Get out of this house!"

A still life in the dark, swirling black tea in a saucer
eyeing your solitary print,
to board the black and white transport
to more substantial time.

In fear, your native tongue,
you proved the best was over
. . . over there, back when . . .

My Aydosha!
She would never live here,
Not even if the rent was free!

Helen on Fire

By morning she slept in
or sipped lukewarm tea.
Only at nightfall would Helen widen her eyes
beneath her long orange weedy hair
and hold court with the neighborhood kids,
most of her own barely visible
as legs on rickety stairs
to the third floor,
a world of blackened linoleum
old fat and the smell of gas
escaping.

Behind us a listless day
of catching bees in bottles
then shaking them till they whirred
into a living machine.
This evening it was Helen on fire.
What you got from Helen
depended on moods
that shot from her like flames.

We stood up close
as she snipped a lock of dull hair
from a runny-nosed daughter,
asking us who had matches to lend her.
Little Roykie, chief inquisitor of bees,
who snared them from hollyhocks
in poorly rinsed picklejars only Dante could do justice to
— *he* had matches to lend her.

As Helen lit the oily wick
the stink of singed hair
curled up and backed us down the stairs;

Ron Charach

I could hear my parents' warning
about Helen and her loose ways
and her endless parade of drunks,
as the cobra smoke infected us
thick and sticky as poverty,
unavoidable as sex.

A smoking bird of ill omen
pursued me
as I tore down those stairs
for the dim yellow porchlights
of my parents' home
where rotting wood got papered over
with a serenity of unmoving flowers
and where nights spent smoldering
were a private affair.

Mr. Adamov

Call me Misha . . .

Saying "Hi, Sir!" to Mr Adamov,
mammoth master in the hallway, a teacher of humanities,
lavishing ideas on anyone who could glimpse his despair.
What slender man could have carried
those enormous checkered three-piece suits,
that authentic gold watch on a chain?
who else anchor a roomful
of posturing kids, straining to keep moving
— with Gulliver and Moby Dick
and the original cast of history.

Having never had the nerve to ask:

An only child of Russian Jews
(he *had* to be an only child)
with one parent as fat, as brilliant, though bitter,
heredity's laws insist bitter . . .
Named "Misha" by an aunt high on poetry,
ambiguous before his first word, a genius
who would never write a book of his own,
too lost in thought to turn his teachings into fame.
He only knew one form of personal gain.

They kept assigning him the enriched class,
a studious pack of wonderkids
who looked down their glasses at those who ran the mile
or tackled muddy dummies at spring training.
Taking on this bookish crew and their single-strand identities,
he refused to give them grades!
But bathed them in the gentle waters of the pass/fail,
encouraging pet projects and walks by the river
so that heart-to-heart talks could crystalize
into missions.

But long after school, his sea of words run dry,
who could he come home to? A family? A wife? A dog?
A cleaning lady who kept him ahead of his sweat?
His politics were left-wing.
Or two elderly parents who refused to look each other in the
eyes.
Afraid of the shower, they lined up their pills like victims,
and prayed that what happened to them in the deathcamps
should never hang over *Our Misha*.
He, watching snowy TV channels over *schnapps*,
She, pasting green stamps in a dimly lit kitchen,
each lying in wait, poised to shoot down initiatives
with *What do you need it for?*

When the weekend arrived Mr. Adamov stayed in bed,
the small of his back pressed to the mattress,
night sweat trapped in the reddened baby folds,
but his mind abuzz with a neon of tunes
for the school's Maytime Melodies,
elegant experiments for the science fair!

He would sooner study someone else's memoirs.

Rolling over on his side, eyes lightly closed,
broad white back to the window, he hummed
an old Hassidic *niggundl*,
and let the human procession
pass him through.

Sea Lotion

Ah, that imported European bracer,
aftershaves from Paris like colognes . . .

Out front the solid stone facade
of the famous McGillivray Block
Syd Schneerson planted a revolving red-and-white pole
and proclaimed the opening of snipping scissors
and the spring of sleek black combs;
where *schmatah business* presidents
could get the fringes trimmed on the busy streets
of their shiny heads, their cigar-stuck faces
fawned by Latino apprentices
cheerfully honing straight-razors

to litanies, batted back and forth
between heavy thrones pumped higher or lower
— "adjusted" — in floor-to-ceiling mirrors:
sports-scores: NFL, AFL, CFL,
AFL-CIO vs. Management,
Tales of horror and delight,
of men and women yielding to body waste
in strange and public ways:
"Piss on him, that bastard!"
"Kahk eem oon!"

"I don't care *how* many camps he survived!"
"Now he *kahks oyf de velt,* that sonafobitch!
Half the models on the street,
real *knock-outs,* with *tzatzkehs* out to *here!*
They drop by to see him, one at a time,
after closing — for *promotions!"*

Restless ringed fingers tapping out
the seething beat of the present
on plush red leather arm-rests
a familiarity of rolled-up sleeves.

Ron Charach

As Moses Goldman, "Maishe," mumbled obscenities
at those who polish the golden Mercedes,
'Syd, believe me, I would never buy
a Krautmobile if it was the *last car* . . . '
"And they have the *nerve* to pull up in them
to *Schul!*
And to let their teenage kids,
— little *pishers* that don't even shave —
race these overpowered death-machines
up and down the Perimeter,
as if life was cheap as *borscht* —"

"But Lemme tell you, there's no place
on this goddam earth, if you'll excuse me, Syd,
where they drive as bad as Boston!"
"Montreal!" from a chorus of traveling salesmen
sharing a life-chair.
"*Shah, Shtiel!* — Boston!* and Boston it will always be.
Not only do they tail-gate halfway up your ass
with their *brights* on, but they expect *YOU* to *pull over
so THEY can speed by! Meshuggah!*"

But someone's beard croaks: *"Manhattan!"*
and what can anyone say . . .
Electric razors switch on to keep the peace
— four, six, eight at a time in the prosperous Sixties,
cascading silvery tufts swept by a colored boy into
gleanings, of men forever wealthy,
the almighty Insured.

Linen hankies pulled out all across town
the day they saw the *CLOSED* sign,
a note taped onto the translucent glass:
that Syd finally had an explosion in his barrel chest
even he couldn't roll with;

cast adrift on that expanding sea
of manicky *entrepreneurs*
whose arteries twist the tap.

Lured you, he did,
by firmly massaging the high-strung cords
at the base of the neck,
just after your whisking, prelude to the talc,
discreetly offering Irish Sweepstakes tickets
and the classical condom, then still illegal . . .
Most of all, with his tonicky man smell
as he leaned his gut against you
to trim those last survivor-hairs up top
he knew to let you keep, antennae,
mementos . . .

And that imported European bracer
in the long-necked green bottle,
aftershaves from Paris
like colognes . . .
made you breathe so deep you almost forgave
those Frenchmen
for being too in love with life
to mess with Nazis —

Ron Charach

A Sparse Oasis

Flying over Jugoslavia, 1945.
They had just salvoed their bombs
(too dangerous to take back)
— with most of them landing
in the middle of a field of sheep,
leaving behind enough mutton
to feed half the German army —

But when the squadron leader announced
his intention to head home over enemy
instead of partisan country, Uncle Dick
respectfully told him
he was crazy.

And when the plane went down,
struck too many times
or run out of gas or luck,
guess whose legs snapped right in half
when he hit the ground,
moaning *"Shit!"* the second he came to.

And then a three-day wait
while the partisans who finally found them
tied a stretcher made of tree roots
and carried him over hill country,
the broken bones grinding away at each other
like testy countries at a border.

He'd already used up his morphine,
but persuaded his buddies in better shape
to part with theirs.
On Day Two-point-something
they slapped on some plaster casts
that had to be cut away
the second they reached the hospital,

a cathedral,
with a male nurse who mumbled *"Christ!"*
at the sight of those lost white legs.

But the surgeon was a spunky guy
who by this-late-in-the-war had seen enough
to have learned a bit. And *he* said:

"Hell, Let's give it a try . . ."

Now, Uncle Dick rolls back his pant legs
like American flags
one at a blessed time
and lets us feel for metal screws and plates
just beneath a sparse oasis
of long black magical hairs.

Ron Charach

Appointments at the Store

Once, Mr. Forzley,
buoyed on an afterchurch drink
told the keeper of his corner store: "Josh,
you should be president
of the United Nations."

Josh, in your two-ocean grocery mart
you carried thick red sides of beef
twice your size;
your wife too; you looked
like something she had budded in her sleep.
Standing tall at five-feet-four in a flood
of hungry customers, you were like granite
weathered by slums,
immigration lines, and an adolescence
spent stacking cans
while other kids sat at streetcorners,
watching girls.
Never needing glasses yourself,
you kept a constant eye on your mirrors;
you could spot a bum and spare him;
talk him out of the store
before he stole.
And you could check the Queen of England's milk.

But your wife's Leah
— her moods could carry,
could skywrite, even after the stormclouds passed
and her week of silence
finally ended.
Then she would inflate with ambition,
water, eyes and cheeks,
bursting with laughter
as she gave away
"our groceries."

The store and your patience
would close
and her doctor was pressed
to do *something,*
mechanical,
electrical
— because who could talk her down
at ninety miles an hour
or drink from overfilled cups of coffee
tasting of detergent?
Her hastily berried face
bloated so full
that all she needed was an hour of sleep
and she could keep the kids up two nights in a row
on songs.
Mr. Forzley said, "Josh,
for sticking by Leah, with the way she gets,
you deserve the Nobel Prize."
And when the phone kept ringing long distance,
he'd console you with,
"Maybe Sweden on the line —?"

Between customers.
sneaking from a half-opened carton of cigarettes
you once caught yourself
in the whirring mirrors overhead,
looking spoon-faced,
one-third the size
of her beehive of hair,
and wondering

if maybe you had all this
coming.

My Third Best Friend

My third best friend could get taken in
by any father who showed promise;
he let older men examine his money
while his own father puttered
in the basement by an open furnace, forging
snake-rings with ruby eyes, remembering
the Germans in both great wars.
He sat through his mother's soliloquies
over dinner, hearing her out with a listless passivity,
a catabolic paleness beyond hurt.
I spent nights with him
in a parked car, with an iridescent flashlight
trying to get him to talk.

One sunny morning I invited
my overcast friend in for coffee.
But when he pulled up his shirt
to reveal row after row of old parents' teeth
still gnawing at his doughy abdomen
I waved Stop! and scrawled
the name of my therapist before passing out
(a best friend's blood can be
especially red)

A Toast to Aunt Leah

Holding the middle-age cocktail, that mix of fatness,
aching joints and despondency,

and remembering you, Aunt Leah,
your weight rising and falling like moods,
your family following . . .
Sweet, the extra sugars in coffees
you brewed for the endless parade:
remote relations, neighbors, neighbors' relatives, familiars
from your sunrise wanderings.
Bitter, the taste of detergent in mugs
hastily rinsed from the last go-round.
But how warm, to be squeezed to your generous breasts,
even if both would come off to cancer.

And your rambling celebratory rhymes,
a Hallmark goodwill for every celebration.
Arriving well ahead of husband and kids,
in an orange blouse and mauve skirt
and a faceful of rouge . . .
How many of us, hearing you practice,
twirled a finger 'round an ear and said,
"Here goes Leah . . ."

How many charities did Uncle have to plead with
to *please* return the cash you mailed?
How many doctors turned incompetent
when all they all ever wanted to do
was commit you?
Many as the plaques layed down
in Uncle's arteries honoring your ventures,
your sudden changes of plans.
Big woman, big heart, big plans.

Great big swooping moods.
We laughed and laughed our hearts out
— at a fifteen-syllable cat —
Regina de la Farbotnik de Catkowitz Da Toid,
at *Pierrot* the budgy, world's best mimic,
who flew wherever-in-Eden he pleased.
How often did you replace them?

But how to replace Aunt Leah . . .
so buffeted by depths, and swells,
then cancer, still deeper depression,
fatness cushioning your tumors
but generosity was not enough;
till finally, a wasting
cancer spreading to the core
of each surprisingly delicate bone.
Then a mental hospital — for you, the world's best spinner
of homilies!

Who else can churn rhymes, Auntie,
who will write *for* us, and *to* us,
and never ever tell on us?

I avoided the hospital.
In your final days you sent out postcards
with flowery poems.
But who could come watch the skull surfacing
in the face of one so provident, now bowed and begging
for something to kill the pain?

"Your children went on to do so well,
You would have had grandsons, such fine grandsons . . ."

Aunt Leah, can I ever live it down?
Must I taste the family cocktail
mixed so terribly strong
for you?

SOMEONE SLIPS IN A FILTER

Summers in the Stairwell

I waited while you twin beauties,
you and your dark sequel of a friend,
sat out your summers in the stairwell
you nicknamed the office;
not knowing you'd made top-secret plans
to laugh off admirers.
How unphased you were, how oblivious to fashion
shrugging off the fear of nuclear war
with fuschia belts over jetblack jumpers
that radiated patterns of the tiniest dots.
And while fashions changed and women grew shoulders
and men lost the ends of their ties
you pitied the other girls who 'had to' stay in step,
frantic young singles clacking overhead,
a stiletto-heeled processional . . .

Today others agree *you* are out of step;
They look into your eyes and sense something missing.
Your friend has been murdered and you laugh alone
at jokes no one else can hear
and all the funny looks they give you.
There are not many like you, oddly distinguished souls
who elude the crush of real events
beneath an iron stairway.

I will visit you one day in some mad collective house
and wait for a rage to wash over you
like a wish, a regret at having lost one who waited
while you giggled away what could have been
my sweetest third of adolescent life.

Ron Charach

In Victor's Parents' Den

Cosy in Victor's parents' den
on a stormy night, Peter Paul and Mary
plaintive on the stereo:
Shoo, shoo, Shoo-la-roo,
Shoo la rack-shack, Shoo-la baba koo,
When I saw my Sally-babby-peel
Come bibble in the bush-eye lorry . . .
lip-synching, ready to cut up the words
as Victor brings down two mugs of steaming tea
and shortbread cookies — on a tray!

deciding not to trash the song
or his feelings

Victor, so red-haired I name him *daucus carotta*
which he accepts with grace,
the only kid my age with nothing to prove,
with a taste for classical music,
the twisted intricacies of foreign tongues.

Would I have enjoyed the evening less
had I known it was something
of a date?

The Last Blind Date

You ran a used love shop with your father —
Royal Doulton figurines and Napoleonna.
Is it fair that you were too Jewish-in-the-wrong-way
too plump too plain too pushy/personal
too urban, spoiled, yet overjoyed
to make a "special salad" for me,
your game plan.
Already I hear uncles scratching at their coffins
Take her! Take her!
Buried in wedges of mushroom and salami and cheese
vinaigrette and garnish for a head
in the professions; I served myself up
in a slow weird way,
played the unhealthy catch, the one to throw back;
said I *had* to take in a horror film after our meal.
Oh, couldn't we do something else!
pleaded the uncles.

To sign on to your archipelago
of romance books, fashions
and programs that mustn't be missed,
the kiss at the door.
I would have had to wait months, according to scruple
for what I never wanted.
For now, the long night-ride home, though free.

Ron Charach

Him, Men

Buxom princess in your twenties
strolling the boardwalk in a bra and thong
bikini — (lingerie-white,
if called upon to testify)
on the run from baby and husband
licking a double-scoop Jamoca Almond-Fudge
and Pralines 'N Cream,
adding softly to your riches.
Oblivious to my plan
to spread my blanket on the sand
wherever you are heading with yours,
whatever beach these long dark legs
deliver you.
To idle the afternoon on that same strip of beach,
— I'll have what *he's* been having —
guiltless behind lightly tinted Foster Grants.
Wonder, if you catch yet another sun-baked head
turreting for peeks:
Is he Foster, is he Grant . . .

Let Daddy worry about your tantrums
and your upkeep, now that you're married
and straddling someone else's
spreadsheets.
Lucky, lucky Daddy;
Finally he's watered down
those pouting-jumpsuit feelings
you could always stir up in him,
men —

Someone Slips in a Filter

Walking the levee with Armand, heading down
a friendship the convention said
was too physical.
Suddenly he heaves a flat rock at *el toro desolato*
and we watch the huge thing rise,
leaving its cocoon of boredom
with a calling up of thighs.
Armand skulks a few yards ahead
and the brush is so thick on either side
all I can do is feel.
He pursues the unlikely ideal, says
a dead mole,
and Armand flips it over with his boot.

"I may never make it
as a writer," says Armand,
"I have too much contempt to describe things."
Someone slips in a filter,
and the farms grow hazy;
conversations we might have had
give way to groans
from the African game farm miles away:
two lions mating.

It is easy to head back
to the warm cabin wood
and the crackling fire,
leaving Armand to think alone in the sunset,
in his mackinaw, jetblack hair and a love affair
with a woman who can lift canoes.
Tomorrow a Dash 7 takes me back to the city.
But tomorrow is many miles away
and the end of the levee is receding
like the climax to our dreams,
and may drag us beneath the horizon
like an avenging mole.

Ron Charach

For Days When We All Are Thin

On these bloated evenings
that fold over on themselves,
I will not take in a single new idea
unless it is accompanied
by pistachios
(and Persian ones at that,
which the Revolutionary Guard
may have tampered with)
unleavened times, when even the sinewy arms
trumped up on highschool monkey-bars
feel tethered
to a fat future.
When enough *will* be plenty.
And I can hand down all the old causes
like tight vests to younger men,
bless their slender hearts and heads.
Lazyboy feet on the Ottoman
a seven-layer Dagwood on rye
by my thickening side,
I lean for the TV and try to follow
who's on first.
Till the sheer load
of just how much I've managed to eat
starts to hit.
Punching out fatty tears
from deep within swollen lids.
Oh for those black-or-white days of 20/20,
days and nights of symmetry
when all wars might yet be ended,
no matter how far away,
no matter how infinite the lines
of ravaging men with black mustaches.
For a time when we all are thin,
like ideals,

thin as the soldier's final gallon of blood
straining to keep his options open;

thinking if not thoughtful times
when the body would serve up its finest juices
to the brain,
as though that crowning place
were the godhead.

Ron Charach

The Mystery Cow

Dining on this wedge, two weeks after Father's funeral,
Who could be hungry at a time like this?
The last of the orphan cowboys,
bought a chunk of rare steer on a seeded bun,
thin steaming shreds
of the mystery cow.
White mayo globbing out,
empty feelings,
suspicious-smelling meat:
Nothing can make it tasty
or safe. But what is a toxin,
only something that makes the body doubt.

Father's last beaten message
from his aluminum coffin:
No more songs out o' me.
Hunger for what can never be resolved,
all the good times
between other sons and fathers.

Never having digested you,
horns and udders, and all,
can I get you to rest
with a good strong heave,
then inter the remains
in a crucible, perhaps on a pedestal,
but far, far away from my food?

To See My Friends

On late autumn nights I risk my car
to see my friends, to unwind
the mountain roads in rain
that transforms the nightscape
to an unyielding glare.
Oncoming brights try to sucker me over
to an elaborate doom.
Inside there are many small green
reassuring dials, a technology that spurns
the low aching wish for completion.
Soon we will complete ourselves,
chart the bloodflow of our very thoughts,
like these thoughts of my friends
that so reliably distract me;
I could be pulled in pieces from the wreck.

Already they have arrived, well ahead of me,
ordering wine while they wait
and wonder what I'll bring along
from this independent life.
They have survived my whims,
have managed a consensus
from some critical percentage
of the rest of my world.
They fought alongside, if not with me
through the body wars
and the teenage fears, jerkily
navigating the thick North American cream.
I've watched them nearly drown,
— still catch them stumbling through circus rings
brought to life again
'by the friendly folks at IBM'
See how they approach whoever ignores them,
with their red bulb noses
and oversize shoes, asking,
'Are *these* our feats?'

We all use the same programs,
have glimpsed far-off foreign lands, and dream
of fanatics marching arm in arm
with photos of some leader
singing about securing the enemy's head
for their leftist or rightist boots.
Somehow I survive them,
even their zealotry.
Does that make me bland and undistinguished,
a man no one would bother murdering,
with emotional shrapnel so gruesome
even an enemy stays away,
to keep his supper down?
Are my nerves all open to the air?
'There is nothing left
worth reproaching!'

Still, at times my friends put on a long look
like refugees who get photographed
but not fed — and call me enemy
for not joining or leaving the cause
or the club, or heeding or flouting
some universal curfew.

Yet every autumn
when the red leaves start to compete with the yellow
for angles in the sun, far too late in my fear, perhaps,
but long before the bright white floods arrive
to reconcile me to solitude,
one more winter-machine,
I risk my car, just to see my friends.

Onionskin

My translucence makes words shimmer
with the delicate originality
of the easily erased.

Whose fragility makes me pray
as I surrender a creasable sheaf of poems
to the thick-waisted manager of the Print Stop
where copies are 15 cents apiece
and small orders get bumped.
Handed over like tissues to a groggy girl-Friday.
He asks her, "How did you run that *last* batch? They're *tilted*."
Does she wonder how, in an ever-expanding universe
she wound up jammed alongside this original?

Though they both have skins, neither seems familiar
with flimsy pages filled with sparse lines.
Do they notice me trembling
at a crimson nail flicking through my papers,
her licked forefinger passing across the page tops;
then a swift march
as she sweeps the odd-lot off the arborite,
nearly tipping a styrofoam cup
stained with lipstick.

Would that they found me unreproducible!
But onionskin is swept away,
as she presses each delicate face to the glass
and the green lights flash
like judgments.
She checks her watch,
gazing past the acoustic tile for lunch
on the horizon,
rear pockets of her bluejeans bulging
as she shifts her shapely weight,

Ron Charach

easing out some early-morning coffee gas
into the huge modern roomful
of machines.

Then remembers me behind her,
thin crescents spreading
along the margins of her ears.
How can I regret that what passes through us,
faint efforts that dissipate and can never be recalled,
except on skin?

Her dark eyes evasive
her cheek slightly warmed,
she bids me farewell,
with "Here's your receipt."

A COSMOLOGY
FOR CAPTIVE
ELEPHANTS

A Cosmology for Captive Elephants

Don't count him in
on any herd activities,
he's a solitaire, belongs inside
a cage of logs, chained to a diamond-shaped rock.
And when the slow cows saunter past
they don't even look at him,
sashaying in their wrinkled houseskins
their young reaching for their teats,
each with the support of five other females,
should he bash his way through,
for a moment of freedom.
But what would such a moment
bring down on him?
Can he approach all six at once?
And what will the feeders and the handlers think:
This bull no longer fears or respects man,
this bull has forgotten the sacred word, "Crush!"
Even the monogastric pellets we feed him
make him restless
when he should be
content.

What kind of life is this? I ask,
watching the night pass,
my wife beside me, so deep in her pregnancy
that I am left worrying for two.
I try to wake back to the world,
to tell her that the new cosmology is fear,
but she rolls over massively
with a drawling "Goodnight, Hon — "
supportive, if entirely asleep.
So I ease back into my pen
of silence and valium,
my tusks going soft, losing air,
my trunk curled up
like a toy.

Ron Charach

A Welder's Dream

A huge chain rises up
through the floorboards
of our personal past,
pulls itself across the room
crushing the pile on the rug as it coils and masses
in this reliquary house.
We watch it, dumb,
the icy links in our breath
a kind of seam
between what is happening
and all we can remember:
a metaphor of days
when you could speculate
on the next world.

You try to reassure me
but the chain lifts its frontal eye
starts to twist around your cool white foot,

when suddenly a huge Cupid comes crashing to the floor.
You call after me: the cold iron
has you trapped, at last.

But I am all truth in the alcove, half out the door.
Without chains, I call back, "I wasn't really born!
I had a mother
who grotesquely overvalued me!"

Alarmed by the squeezing and retching
while the metal has its way with you
I dream of golden rings, spinning into spheres,
just like the harmless ring
you insisted I buy you.

A Marriage with Children

A marriage with children is worth

the endless procession
of meal after meal,
imperceptible segments
of the gigantic flesh-colored worm,

. . . the need to think about food,
to cut and slice and rewarm
then eat while you feed
and clean up while you supervise
the child's play of others; and then
the need to plan the next meal . . .

makes the biggest meal yet
of your time,
for that's what family

feeds on.

Ron Charach

On the Working Farm

I take Samuel, our youngest, to the working farm
and stop us in front of the pigsty
(a big mistake)
this lanky *Oklahoma* type
keeps whacking the rear
of a huge sow
trying to back her up
so the boar can make his move.
"That's the daddy pig," I say,
but the Okie slides open the muddy gate
for the boar to muscle into position;
makes his sudden mount, our visiting eyes
wider than his swinging black bag,
his unsheathed poker
disappointing —

As we back away
into the hay-reeking barn,
there's another massive sow, she and her piglets
held in separate stalls,
but within ear-splitting range of each other,

so the piglets squeal to heaven
when they smell her, and she heaves
against the rough planks
trying to silence
their chorus of hunger.
The second this tumult strikes
the reverberating key
of history,
Samuel looks up into my eyes.

Waterlines

Holding my baby daughter
as she squirms and chortles
in the chest-high water of the sheltered bay,
her softness up against me, nothing is
but the soft slap of waves
and a fade of others playing —

Soon we'll be blending with the Sunday evening blur
of red tail-lights snaking back to Metropolis;
we'll stop off after sunset at the burger assembly
waiting for the traffic to thin,
other families pulling up in campers,
their two-year-olds in trances, fathers so weary
they throw their car keys
in the trashbin.

Back on the highway I watch her
in the mirror, my darling little charge
content in her custom seat
even as the deerfly bites start swelling
under her soft cotton shirt.
Finally she surrenders,
and will miss the last hour of our journey.
This dark, it is my own more than hers.
Hers is a more perfect skin
flawed only by vaccination;
though there is none
against what lurks
in the long cold waters.

Ron Charach

Water Sport

Like when you're taking sun
by a dreamy blue lake
And suddenly a speedboat
fractures the scene
pulling some long-haired goof
in a tube, screaming
"Yaaa-hooooo!"
and though his legs are shut tight
three quarters of a gallon of lake
shoots up his bottom
as he goes —

You gaze into the waves,
then the ripples
the boat leaves behind,

and the departure of the noise-machines
makes you an old lake turtle
stretched out on a rock,
your neck surprisingly long,
with no intention
of surprising
anyone.

Fishing

a small specimen
hooked and torn on
rival curiosities

Gone Fishing with three and five-year-olds
for four-inch stickleback bass
lounging in the shadows under a dock
at Lake of Bays.
Little Jonah dangles a mini-rod,
a baitless hook without barbs;
for an hour he's watched the older kids reel
and throw back a dozen live ones.
Decides to sink his little line
into our pail of silently wriggling
captives awaiting release;
to be a big fisherman
in a small pond; at age three
even a Simple Simon routine will do
on the road to male bonding.

Most of the captured fish
are none the worse for wear
by the time we throw them back;
a sunfish flashes a shimmering golden-orange belly
to warm a vegetarian's heart. But then:
one of the bass has *swallowed* a hook
and in the process of *un*hooking him
— a disemboweling!
We discard the evidence,
though the moment he hits water
he lists to one side
(the kids don't seem to notice)
leaving a thick smell of entrails
on top of the fish skin smell on my gripping hand
now more murderous than sporting.

Ron Charach

But we're up in Muskoka,
with a fifteen-dollar rod Morty bought
at Canadian Tire,
and he shows me how to unhook a fish
as it twists and tries to wriggle free
without scratching up my hands
or being a fool in front of
the kids.
(My own dad would never have
shelled out money for worms,
could no more have taken a life
than saved one.)

With the boys clutching their rods
reeling in the inevitable worm
of enforced silence, an Irish nanny approaches
and exclaims,
"If *anything* ever grabbed
the other end of that line,
I know *I* should die of fright!"

After Religious School

Orbiting the ivy-covered Temple
two hundred parents in Volvos,
Jeeps and mini-vans descend
to claim precious cargo.
The soot has finally been scoured
from the northwest wall of the school,
reminder of the fire that thankGod no man kindled,
an accident of drawings
on a hot rad.

A kaleidoscope of snowsuits
pours into the center hall!
So many sizes of color-coordinated kids;
bandy-legged boys in team hats,
socially practiced girls in Indian braids
or the flouncy ponytails of braids
recently untied — some
wearing a splash
of coppery freckles!

The joyous clamor of these getaways
makes me forget the waif
who lives above the chicken 'n rib shop,
who each day must smell the food
his mother can buy only
a few times a year.
Though a swirl of autumn leaves about the stone steps
reminds of the coming of pagan Hallowe'en,
with its universal access
to the sweet.

Ron Charach

How adorable, Dear Lord, your Torah
when we no longer need die for it,
or dance on it for sadists.
How precious, these children
who have learned to love to read,
who we can finally
afford to feed.

A Brief Secular History

The wife, far less Jewish than I,
forces me on a journey
to Bathurst and Eglinton
to stock up for our *seder*.
My assignment is *Nortown*.
"All you need to know," she says,
"is that as you come in,
the deli is on your right,
and the dairy on your left"
(though you have to do a Christopher Columbus
around a store packed with people
to discover the check-out,
after waiting in the longest line
since the line-ups to leave Spain).
All for a booty of "six or seven large
salt-and-pepper *gefilte* fish,
and eggs" (for boiling)
"with a late expiry date."

But when I arrive
the store *is* the line-up
from the moment I enter;
not a single push-cart left.
The one my hands head for
belongs to someone else,
and she lets me know it.
Just ahead of me, a dapper shrunken lady
with a small gray head looks up
and says, "I've been pushed out of lines
three times today, and I won't let
it happen again." But then she smiles,
and confides to me, and two others behind me,
"You know, Honey, I had a stroke
just last year, and lost all my languages.

Ron Charach

But ThanksGod, my daughter
is a psychiatrist — at Western — and she set me up
with a speech — what do you call them? — pathologist, yes,
thank you . . ."
But we're waved ahead with a "*Who's next!*"
so I never learn her daughter's name.

What an assortment of *lantzmen!*
their shopping-carts bulging with blood-red briskets
and slabs of fish to be *gefilte*'d.
Dark-haired men, some handsome,
very occasionally tall,
and so many in bulky, soft Italian leathers.
Old *greeneh* ladies
in mothbally overcoats,
who find the prices painful;
but beside them,
lavish young doctors' daughters
in designer cottons.

Such beauties!
some natural, others thankful to their surgeons
for whittling away the Streisand look;
spending their fathers' fortunes
with the vengeance of children
of workaholics,
milking every last skin pore
of impurity, painting
all twenty nails!
Some are shorter, thicker, born-to-be-squat,
yet bravely sticking to their diets,
even in this oasis of carrot-raisin *tzimmahs*
and (God forgive your children)
Kol Esterol fare,

like that polyfilla of the vessels,
chopped liver.
Here and there are women too well-schooled to push
for foodstuffs,
who *keep* the steely gray in their hair, and take courses
at university (always a suburban University)
in sociology or art, or the sociology of art.
(Somewhere in the downtown university
a dinosaur who roared about quotas on Jews
still stalks the dim halls
in tenured shoes,
with a long tail of crisp last names
wound tight around the family tree
he always drags with him.)
Those who push *here, just off Bathurst*
are only fending
for their families — against genetic memories
of bread lines, soup lines,
line-ups to get the right papers,
to forge papers,
line-ups to make bribes for exit-visas
— *Selektion* lines —
These are the lines
that make everyone tense
and in a hurry.

Finally, I arrive
at the check-out line,
the one you can see the street from,
two bent old ladies ahead of me help each other
count change.
When a graying, professorial man my age appears
— out of line — a 15-pound turkey in his arms.
"Is this the end of the line?" he asks,
and of course it's not.

I risk the wrath of those behind me
and give him cuts, saying loudly,
"Come on in; you have a burden,"
knowing no one will challenge a slavery theme
with only a day left
till *Pesach*.

As the noise-level rises,
I feel closer to my people,
the way I rarely do in a synagogue;
By the time it's my turn at the register
I don't really
want to leave.
Though in minutes I'm in the store next door,
lined up again,
this time for *Leiberman's Splendid Chocolates*
and a déjà vu:
Mr. Leiberman, gaunt for a chocolates-man,
handling the most demanding line
in the diaspora, with bald-headed Viennese
civility.
So, when an impatient lady snaps,
"Did you forget my other two boxes?"
he says sweetly, "No, Madame.
They are just now being wrapped."
She reddens, just the slightest bit,
then adds, "Thank you,
you are very kind."

She might have said "splendid."

Distances across the Sink

The cupboards are as bright as a hospital,
an enamel white on white,
but behind them is a scurrying world of legs
the industrial spray can't reach.
Nothing changes:
Stone goblets fill with mould,
the nozzle still freezes like a cobra
in a kitchen dream
of an abandoned sink.
On the dishrack lie two
discolored hands,
a butter knife running rust,
two Visigoth chalices
and a steel-gray plate.
In our lives:
a distance,
my dishes stacked separate from your own,
my parents' cutlery, in the pattern
you have come to hate;
some tupperware spheres you introduced
that I am too far gone to criticize.
We always pushed for a shared sink;
then we switched off the lights
and we waited.
One morning of early sunlight streaming in
may our devotion to the unnatural
gleam —

Ron Charach

Off Somewhere Blowing

When you picked me up on the infinite roadway,
the Annex popping up on either side
I'd been running, breathing the same steam we all know
from the night film.
Don't be afraid of a man without callouses
in a linty black coat
with midnight eyes.

'Are you still *really* married?' I asked myself,
and had to answer 'No.'

And we drove around so many hours
comparing the aluminum siding of our relationships,
that you passed my place
and headed us for yours —
But, then, "I miss my wife, sometimes," I said,
and you braked, and said, "You *do*."
So you let me out on the snowed-in roads
and I watched you pull away, a bold red dot receding,
Searching the icy horizon for signs of security;
but he was off somewhere, blowing on his aching hands
coming out of a handgun dream he could never share.

The Art You Could Not Buy

My wife has filled our lonely hours like stomachs;
her heart can now lean back and stop trapping jesters.
Deep within the yellow fat her ventricles pucker and relax,
pucker and relax at the sound of me
saying things.

No man ever fell into her soupy eyes for nothing.
Who could miss the hours she lops off
from an already shortened day?

My wife says, "No man *really* knew me before you."
But she winks in the steamy mirror, unwinding
from her plush lilac towel, a post-opera presentation.
She is the surgeon sent to work on my face,
to till my inner acrylics; she can suction out
alternate endings,
pull me through the operation.
"Treat your life like the art you could not buy," she says.
"Treasure what we build
as if you were the one who could do
the enjoying.

Let's be content to copy the originals —"

EATING
HOUSES

Doing Well in the Restaurant

Doesn't our love do well
in the restaurant, by candlelight
with other people feeding us,
the easily stripped decor,
the Spanish waiter who would understand
my slapping his face
if the cork were incomplete —
Don't we fare well on the long ride home
singing in the backseat,
a rolled five assuring a goodnight from the cabbie
who reluctantly pulls away . . .
Would we deserve any less
if we cut our bitter cord
and you were free to pay your debts
to the men you no longer see
since me?

"Should we be acting this way — so early?"

Let's ask our waiter
when we've ordered the cocktails
he swears are required.
How can he refuse us, on a Monday night
if we stare into his long black eyes
the next time he approaches
and plead,
"Tell us nothing but
the specials —"

Ron Charach

Eating Houses

House of Steaks

Into
the fabled dining house of two rooms
whose manager tried to go out of business
but was bought out by his own clientele,
forced to stay open for unparalleled steaks.
Where you are serviced by waiters so friendly
they almost notice you're there,
plunking down plastic bowls, a flask of oil,
a flask of vinegar — "You mix" —
with cunning food familiars . . .
They serve up the prime steak naked,
filet or New York strip,
meat it is not legal to buy at Loblaws,
meat the poor will never encounter
even in their choicest dreams . . .
They serve it without fanfare
or so much as a sprig of parsley,
in this meat-eater's paradise
graced by the rich and the bitchy
who find the portions skimpy in nouvelle cuisine,
who like to eat Chinese,
but have a primal need
for steak and potatoes . . .

But I have the worst seat in the house
facing the open door to the kitchen,
a toothless old crone moving back and forth
with a scalding pot, in some sort of kitchen-help hat.
My choice of views:
four sullen and identically Spanish-tempered
Chinese waiters, standing at the back
waiting for Visas,
red linen over their arms concealing weapons;

a smoky aquarium of long-tentacled lobsters
climbing over their rich brothers,
deliberate as tanks,
while a silver-haired man watches one
getting hauled out, and demands,
"Did you weigh that in or out of the water?"
And a large-lettered illustrated sign
about what to do if you choke.

From my wife's better view
loom sullen wrought-iron pastoral lanterns
suspended from an unadorned ceiling of acoustic tile,
hanging against walls as red as blood.
And a circular bar with a TV — for those lining up
(there are no reservations) — gives the place
a seedy Vegas feel.

Double-taking on the menu, or gaping
at the parade of furs in the coat-check room
that would make a robber forget about the register;
till the Advent: an enormous sixteen-ouncer
of charred meat, beneath a mountainslide of onion rings
and Idahos sliced tightly,
still in their skins . . .

You can almost hear arteries closing
as you polish off your plate. And later, prime burps
that help you remember the meal, like an idea
mulled over . . .

For dessert we watch four or five beefy men
looking like Norman Mailer bringing in his mother,
scowling their way past the unmoving line;
assorted species of WASP, more likely would-be WASPs
savoring the steak smells like country-club air.

And though none can join the Granite Club,
and have family sitting it out back home
in Russia, or in suburbia, with changed last names
that won't close doors to university,

they seem to not notice us
or the sleeping baby we brought with (we mistook
the House for a family eatery).
A single glance from them could warn us
just how deep into the shadows
of these meaty urban hills
we've dared to venture
this time.

A Parts of Chicken Place

People are ashamed to be caught here,
a parts of chicken restaurant
for those still hanging from a branch
of the middle class.
Bathed in the cloy of a dozen orange lamps
our faces diffuse in false subtlety.
Young bachelors are everywhere,
with a "fill 'er up" approach to supper,
bolting this approximation of barbeque
like they can't wait to pay the cheque
and be back outside
the windows.
Senior citizens, in pairs when they're women,
squinting for exact change
as if plastic had never been invented.
Here and there foot soldiers of high finance,
assistants to the assistant, loan officers,
real estate lawyers doing badly,

accountants who know a good deal
when they eat one;
lots of steno types from fishing hamlets Out East
come to dig for gold on their lunch breaks
in Toronto.

Then in he walks
and thickens the air —
a lean bachelor in his thirties
(he must be a bachelor)
half his face frozen to a grimacing mask,
holding a withered arm across his chest
while his good hand deliberates
with a cane.
Sits in the booth straight across from us!
— in a restaurant half the size of a football field.
He gets no favorite waitress
because the one who ends up serving him winces
when he asks her to butter his roll
and stir in his dressing.

Our children stare
for us and watch him negotiate
the single choice you never need a knife for,
(this overcooked chicken shreds off the bone
with the slightest pressure) — it tears
like the very fiber of those
who would eat it.
Makes us take stock
of our luck with the body while it lasts;
we prod it like a side rib, a back rib,
like the tough-looking black rib
you bypass, for something
succulent.

Convince us, heart,
that this is yet food;
that we might make it for ourselves,
even for guests;
that the first famished bite
may yet justify the rest.
That the men and women who eat here
— the regulars —
though they have no family nearby
and may never start their own,
will forever remain
worth cooking for.

A Mock Air Raid

South Florida.
Into this landscape of overgrown houseplants
that turn dimensional at night
lie estates that lure you nowhere
down narrow roads between steep canals
that celebrate the water table all year round.
Between the retirement centers where golf is life
stand little roadside Florida cracker huts
now selling greasy snacks instead of moonshine.
Signs on sinking stilts line the road: Oreo Seafood.
First Swamp Baptist, presided over
by the Reverend Upthegrove.
Taking his sweet time up the road
is a white brushcut of a man with a scrawny
sunburned neck, in a rusted-out Ford
with a bumper sticker that reads,
"I'm the N.R.A. and I vote!"
You want to run him into one of them 'gator ditches
while he doesn't have his rifles handy.

Not like the cop at the Wynne-Dixie
where they all wear guns
'cause the place stays open all hours
and even the largest American flag in the world
— big as the one on Okeechobee at Military Trail —
has been stolen from its flagpole twice.

"Why be afraid of extraneous life?"
asks your parents' unweeded lawn, yielding
to surprise shoots of gumbo-limbo
and the colonizing banyans.
They don't try to keep South Florida under control,
but allow in the colorful crotons,
Cubans who take refuge behind functional chain fences,
Nicaraguans who hide out in churches,
drug smugglers who regularly weed their clientele,
and French-speaking gangsters from Montreal.
Even the roaches fit in nicely,
are dubbed "palmetto bugs"
and patrol their own little ghettos in the kitchen
or under the great hallway bookcase
of American classics.
Only get stomped on if they pass a certain size;
and when you switch on a light in any room
you know to look away first.

They live near Palm Beach Airport, so near
that the landings rattle every windowpane,
keep the roaches doing the samba.
'Course when it's not too hot they close the windows
and muffle the sonic booms;
and the take-off and landing routes vary
with the winds. Not that it's endless,
since they don't start earlier than seven a.m.,
and the last ones leave by eleven at night
or else face hefty fines.

And there are also trains,
tooting horns as they pass by
— till I tell your folks their home is a theme pavilion,
on transportation.
What can they answer, but remind me
that our kids get a kick out of the racket,
at least in the daytime.
Why need they apologize, these scientists
who respond to insect life with tupperware
rather than chemicals, and to high-crime downtowns
by confining their walks.
Two gray panthers, each with an advanced degree
and the fully grown-up family — all doing well.
They still head off to work each day
and when Maggie comes home she cooks for us all
while we tend our kids
and Bernie sharpens knives.
After a rare meal of leftovers
the suppers are getting so good again I ask her:
"What do you do when you run out of surprises?"
And she answers, "Why, I just start right over."
Like NASA — only decent, Americans
who were angered and afraid
when their neighbors voted Reagan.
You have to bury people like these
before you fully appreciate . . .
They wouldn't have it any other way;
though Maggie's got her eye set on cremation,
with her ashes spread across the forests
of upstate New York
where there are real deciduous trees
that nurtured a few hundred years' worth of Warings,
with every one of them accounted for!
She thinks the laws against scattering remains by plane
are silly.

When our vacation's up we leave them, these experts,
to play out their sunset years in the jetstream,
those 747's raising Bernie's pressure, not his voice . . .
We always feel vulnerable without them
for at least a week,
our own jungle more or less completely
paved over.

Most of all we miss their silvery hair,
in which gradually the grey transforms
to luminescent white
whenever you talk with them
at night.

HECLA
ISLAND

Hecla Island

What travelers will remember
is the road,
the would-be ancient causeway
that reformed the islanders
of their isolated ways.
Unreal as privacy
built in '71,
it rolled the world in all year round;
though the portion that is paved
like a high-tech pier through the town
is less than a half-mile long.
Visitors scratch up their wagons and vans
just getting there, a vague initiation
to what is never really entered.

Sixty families
forced to move back to the mainland
in the early '70's; now
five remaining pastel buildings
are supposed to make you think
of Iceland.

"Somehow it isn't
what I'd *expected*."
I heard you out
as you panned it,
propped on an elbow in bed,
Disappointment
in Lake Winnipeg's largest island
"that boasts a rugged shoreline,
rich in moose and a vast array
of waterfowl,"
pelicans and heron
where they just couldn't be.

I began to worry you were right,
that from the vast human overlook
it's always too early or too late
to see the deer.

Remember that vacation
when we put so much repellent on
that no one came near us?
That's the way we want it,
tight control
over who puts the bite on us
for company.
Long after you fell asleep
I sat up in the cottage living-room
of darkly stained paneling
and second-rate furniture;
every few minutes a new kind of bug
would shoot in.
Now a dusty miller
ricocheting in the tunnel of light,
now an insect so small
it could only be guessed at
by its flying lanes.
Always the spiders in waiting
who see in every housefly
a dark beefy round,
finding the mosquitoes quite bony
but for the warm squirt of blood in them.

How many were dispatched by two-way radio
from the "managed marsh,"
their homes paved over
when the highway came in?

I have never been moved by those Morrisseaus
that show the mosquito as a god
six times the size of a canoe,
though an endless supply of them
would drain in courage
what it left behind in blood.
I remain a "single mosquito man,"
one mosquito per sensitive man,
and the moment one comes into view
I understand:
This is what my two-year-old means
when he pulls at his ear:
something very strange
has been happening — *here,*
some high-pitched whine
there will never be a word for.

Just one of these can burst through
the membrane of my dreaming.
Impossible to spot on busy sheets
and no point trying to kill
on a shag rug;
but it's four a.m., too dark to search
these rosy-brown walls.
Mercy on my half-acre forehead
you microthing,
you hovering siphon, weightless
yet so able to take off anyway.
But here comes the little bastard
to bite me *again!* Circling —
my personal mosquito, likes my taste
but is unimpressed
with my defenses,
a random swatting and waving about
of tormented Kong hands.

Still less with the cartoon of me
fumbling for a flashlight
or the dresser lamp
— attract in more if I have to —
but the only way sleep will ever come
is if I finish off
this one.

In the domestic dark of the cabin
my wife sleeping ruthlessly well,
faint rustlings come
from my son's room
and jar me from reading
about forces that torture
but are only obeying orders.
All I dare do
is stand
and face the blackened hall,
stomach muscles tightening
to a small round mirror.
Entering the bathroom
— a little bit closer —
I pull it out, thinking,
What manner of beast would harm
a mildly pissing man?
and watch a daddy-long-legs slowly climb
through the unpredictable
groaning.
Go to bed;
never mind what's in the next room.
What if the boy is sprouting talons?
Or rushes out to greet me
with much older eyes?

Let the dawn arrive
and such things dissolve
on their own . . .

Next morning,
the cottage reclaimed from the ether,
my wife tells me our son
somehow wriggled out of bed
and slept half the night
with his head under a chair.
"What if he'd woken up
and hit his head!"

How to tell her
that faint rasping breath
on a night out at Hecla
— from a creature
sharing my toothbrush —
had me riveted.
Tell her of islands I head to
when she falls asleep and leaves me
to my cycles;
narrow escapes to a land
where night-fearing souls
transform themselves
to minds that buzz like bulbs,
minds so knowing
no devil would come
within a book of them.

Ron Charach

Overcast at the swimming-hole
I walk into the chilling waters,
looking too much myself
stepping on the sharp rocks,
and think of men and women
who retire from life
to articulate their pain.
Treading towards the orange buoy
so far out and ablur
I shrug the urge to fail,
to sink,
and start committing
the awkward stroke
that always takes me farther
than it has the right to.
Mid-way my temples sound
the recognition:
This water is not feeling any warmer.
Still I head out,
trying to warm a mind with a body
of sheer activity,
a witness to catastrophe
who is no longer needed
because there are so many others.

Then catch glimpses
in the lake of shadows
— of a face — another,
then a long thin arm
— a woman's? — a man's?
Could it be Hopkins or Hardy
or Dickinson,

whipping white light
out of the cold grey waters?
To swim out alongside them,
even for a moment,
even struggling —

THE FARE
TO TRENTON

"*Brenda, Brenda, It's OK!*"

Brenda laughing out of control
as Ma reaches into the bag of potatoes
and starts heaving them at Pa,
(good old
good-for-nothing
drunk)
But they've *both* been at it,
Ma taking off before Pa can retaliate,
but five minutes later stumbling right back in,
having wrapped Pa's pick-up truck
around a post.
Then it's Brenda's turn
to leave the whole damn
screaming mess,
kid-brothers and sisters and all —
She plans to cut through the cornfield
and walk along the highway
to the first farmhouse with lights on.
But halfway out into the windy night,
the sky black with clouds,
the farmhouse lit up with screams
that lose their edges
in the prairie distances,
she hears Pa calling out,
"Brenda, Brenda, it's O.K.!
You come home!"
So she gives away her position
in the field,
and stands up to show Pa
where he can find her.
Then hears it whizzing by.
Starts running, as though she'll never
turn around again,
as though Mother weren't calling:
"MyGod! MyGod!"

and winds up spending
her first full night ever
away from home.

Years later,
Ma and Pa divorced,
with Pa remarried and mellower,
and off the vodka for good
because of ulcers,
even the grandchildren can get away
talking back to him,
and poking fun at his Old Country ways.
To this day Brenda hasn't brought up
"that time with the rifle"
with anyone.

*"And it's all
just as well."*

What You Need To Know

They both saw me off at the station
though Father's wheelchair embarrassed me.
Mother was full of seeing-you-off.
Father had the usual aphasia:
A Dis! A Dis!
He used to warn me to stay away from 'The Garden.'
It's full of vegetables, he'd say.
*Those geezers will point so hard at a thing
that the name falls off;
then even YOU can't remember what the damn thing's called.*
Now he just waved his polystyrene what's-its-name
as Mother handed me a cheque, to his cooing:
A Dat! A Dat!
His eyes welling as he saw me take it.

She whispered something
which passed over me,
said it in the whisper
of somebody bathing me.
Also, it was the first time I'd noticed
she was getting fat —
still pretty, but fat.
The weight Dad was losing from his arms
and legs was being grafted up along her sides.
She also gave me some quick advice about food,
about how too slim was no good either.

Auntie Minta would have come
but she had metastases,
and Arnie once said
she made our Dad look good.
It bothered me,
that she fancied herself good at dying.
I would've jumped for those trainlights
right then and there
but I could almost hear Mom on suicide,

holding forth like a large stuffed bird;
and Dad gaping at the red and white smears
along each track, cooing:
A Dis an' a Dis an' a Dat!

Remembering: The First Round

1977. In a non-teaching hospital.

On rounds with the staffman,
a nice enough guy in his own way,
at the bedside of a twenty-six-year-old man
with a mustache — clearly gay,
weak, and looking up at us in fear
because we are about
to discharge him.
He has night sweats, really bad ones,
is losing weight
and has a golf ball in each groin.
But all the fancy tests we run
come out negative;
he's been in hospital a week,
and his biopsies haven't told us much.
"I can't go home like this;
I'm dying!" he rasps.
But the senior staffman shakes his head (we're sorry),
and on our way out whispers, "This guy's a *faygel."*
(Yiddish for "a birdie,")

Remembering his pale, sweaty face,
those painful groins, and the terror in his eyes —
the staffman's unswerving calm, even levity
as the Specter of AIDS — *who could imagine*
the span of its mantle —
passed over us,
having made a first-round
selection.

Ron Charach

Pathology Gives Us a Class Called Pots

What a company of diseases: the great imposter Syphilis
with his crew of clown nasties:
Gumma, Chancre, Snuffles, and 'Satellite' Bubo . . .

Pathology gives us a class called pots.
We set down our pens to pass around small packages
with plastic bubble domes, warily,
lest they leak.

Inside each, some ragged organ that has failed;
here an adrenal gone lumpy, there a kidney
milky orange and shredded by a crumbling tumor
that long ago surpassed its size.

Too small these worlds of flesh aswim
in formalin, faint clouds condensing
to obscure the histories —

Young student, we the dismembered
were also part of life. The liver packed
inside this bubble belonged
to the through-with-thrashing husk
of a day-old babe.
Packaged by some curatorial eye
may we still serve as reminders
of a world where men must act
when God refuses —

Come closer to the acrylic, closer
to life's delicate machinery.
Tonight, marvel at
your lover's wondrous casing,
even as her upstretched arms
make small imperfect domes
of her breasts —

In Dark Tangled Woods

In dark tangled woods the burnt man stalks me,
his parched hand tracing my silhouette.
But watch his onion head unravel and blow
across the field like so many cartoons
once I'm safe inside your Tudor home.
There we extract the stings of disaster
and dine on a hash of midnight fears.
I serve up chunks of hairy meat
from the burnt man and the blue man
and even Mr. Green. (You burp
and reswallow).

By eight a.m., only fifty minutes later, I have used
your brawny reasoning to clear a corridor through life.
Leaving you to your hazy calm, your quaint sense
of boundaries, I take my first steps
into the morning glare; then I wonder
how you manage.

Do you nap through the worst parts,
when dark blue shadows and a sudden hand
raise the hairs along your neck?
And in your long nights alone, amid echoes
from all three levels of your widower house,
your children having left so long ago,
soul after soul coming
only to unburden,
How is it that you manage?

Ron Charach

Papa John Union

This was my very first telegram:
The operator swore and the woman
said my name was wrong.
My first guess was
Stockholm trying to reach me for the Prize;
call this mental health.
But by the time I could answer
Western Union had gone home
to his kids, to brush his teeth in a ranch-house
where generations in yellow raincoats
work the welcome-mats (with yachts).

Now that the barbecue is canceled
food must be processed indoors:
Chip Union brings in the DANGER fluid
and helps Dad prime the water;
the pollution device, Old Uncle Rex with the bad heart
of gold, is kept far away from the microwave.
And though Chip won't read in public,
he makes a sign for every type of food brought in,
while the churlish Mason-Dixon cousins drawl
their guesses: "Mai-ize?"

At eight p.m. Western Union goes back on line
— that means my message too.
Papa John Union pours his fifteenth beer,
still half-full on the table, saying,
"My heart is a speck-tator of long distant messages."
Then his whole family files past a kiss
— everyone is careful not to leave.

The Fare to Trenton

There are parts of my brain identical to Trenton,
where an emotion would get run off the circuit.
Trenton, Paramus, Passaic, Hoboken,
quarters in a common lobe of industry,
the Industrial Grays, with their German timing,
their pride in the central team of bee-cells,
storing each drop of unused juice
even as boilers stoke the basement
of the crocodile cortex, straining
to let the machinery rip —

He hesitates, pale and afraid of the commuters,
his wet eyes reflecting an identity
that hangs on a single overvalued idea,
his sense of right and wrong long ago replaced
by the fear of another's hand striking him.
Before we arrived he was alone
in the hollow train station,
checking telephones for quarters,
making faces in the photo-booth,
dreaming of a second coming,
curled up on the wooden benches
to the rumble of trains.

In my small black bag, a syringe and two vials.
I watch him sleeping, then check the time
— an unpleasant task.
Two attendants wait under the great cigaret clock;
there's a men's room a good fifty feet away.
I rehearse an introduction: "We're only here
to help you . . . There's no way we would hurt you . . ."

Ron Charach

and think of religious orders, silent monasteries
that made do with whatever thin selves
arrived at their doors.

Have to help as many as I can
generate that costly Trenton fare.

EPILOGUE

Colonoscopy

What could be cleaner or merrier than to sweep off
a dusting of snow on a crisp sunny day?
But this morning I visit the Rudd for routine colonoscopy.
Two days ago at the pharmacy I joked about my purchase —
two clear bottles of Citromag and three tins of egg-nog
    Ensure —
"I'm going to a really wild party!"
"Yeah, right!" laughed the pharmacist.
It won't be a picnic.

There is something cleansing
about volunteering. Something reassuring about knowing
exactly how much waste *this* body can contain.
And the brochure, praising courage, reassures:
the laxative is the worst part.

Unseemly, to talk about fires raging out of control
on an area no bigger than a quarter,
to draw more attention there than you have to.
But by the morning of the test I wonder
if I'll ever sit again.

Today I am to know myself
better; insights
ten years of psychotherapy
can't provide.
To plumb the inner furrows and folds
in search of some polypy Jabberwock
to ensnare and burn away.

The clinic is a field of a room sectioned off
with plush furniture in themes of brown and off-white
on a carpet the color of toast.
A nurse in crisp white uniform
hands out the inevitable forms.

Ron Charach

I write down practically nothing:
as a teen some "irritable bowel" (whatever that means),
but then add: *Mother died of cancer of the coecum.*
Dispassionate faces in the waiting room;
some have been through this many times.
At forty I'm here early, more imagining than ill,
but across me sits a black-haired youth with a colitis look,
his face grey as ash, his mother wearing a worried look.

Yet I am chosen first,
and am soon up on a tilting table,
having passed on the sedation,
(at three o'clock, I have patients of my own to see).
"That's my finger," says the good G.I.,
calling to mind more than one off-color joke,
and in an instant, he launches
five feet of limber, greased technology
as I try to relax and be a good sport.

(Two weeks earlier,
a friend of mine went
to have a hemorrhoid lanced:
benevolent Chinese specialist
in Hirohito glasses;
anaesthetic injected: *ouch!*
infused, but *OUCH!* at the scalpel swipe,
the prostrate one tightening up
fighting back with his only bit
of available muscle
as above his shoulder, the doctor starts to shriek,
"You oppose me! You oppose me!")

Forget such stories, in the name of deep breathing,
in the name of hatha-yoga,
relaxation therapy;

as a million dank villous fingers clamp down
to slow its progress,
and are promptly overruled.

But negotiating the great splenic bend is more than I bargained
for.
I grow shocky, *"If it's all going to be like this, then I quit!
Is it too late for sedation?"*
But the nurse pats my sweaty back,
the sleek craft noses deeper into inner space.
Suddenly I feel for *"the Pain is Real"* victims,
for the gaunt young man in the waiting room
flipping through *New Yorker* cartoons for answers;
for abandoned old duffers everywhere
curled up on their cots,
muttering —

But relief comes quick to the healthy;
turning over
for the transverse portion of our journey
things start to ease up, even as the air shoots in
so the man can do what he's paid to —

We're finally in the coecum; for he asks the nurse
to "wiggle the coecum," (*my* coecum) — another new
    experience.
This is the place that killed my mother;
I hold my breath; what if he lingers . . .
"Hmmm," he says, "let's give this lens a wash."
But soon we're on our way out to brighter land,
where we need no fiber-optic light,
and corners are turned easily.
A wad of kleenex is left in place
for the mopping up.

"I'm sorry if I gave you a rough time," I say
getting dressed
in my propriety.
"Oh, I think it was *us* who gave *you* the rough time," he replies,
then announces,
"You're clean."